YOUR MONEY AND YOUR LIFE

The Living as a Christian Series

Basic Christian Maturity

Growing in Faith
Steve Clark
Knowing God's Will
Steve Clark
Decision to Love
Ken Wilson
God First
Ken Wilson
Sons and Daughters of God
Ken Wilson
Growing Closer to God
Tom Gryniewicz
Your Money and Your Life
Ken Wilson

Overcoming Obstacles to Christian Living

How to Repair the Wrong You've Done
Ken Wilson
Getting Free
Bert Ghezzi

The Emotions

Facing Your Feelings
Bert Ghezzi
The Angry Christian
Bert Ghezzi
The Self-Image of a Christian
Mark Kinzer
Living with a Clear Conscience
Mark Kinzer
The Fear Factor
Jim McFadden

Christian Character

Strength under Control
John Keating
How to Become the Person You Were Meant to Be
Peter Williamson

Personal Relationships

Taming the Tongue
Mark Kinzer

Your Money and Your Life

Ken Wilson

SERVANT BOOKS
Ann Arbor, Michigan

Published by Servant Books
P.O. Box 8617
Ann Arbor, Michigan 48107

Cover photo by John B. Leidy © 1983 Servant Publications
Jacket and book design by John B. Leidy

83 84 85 10 9 8 7 6 5 4 3 2 1

Printed in the United States of America
ISBN 0-89283-171-5

Acknowledgements

Much of the material in this book is derived from a teaching developed by Ralph Martin. Readers familiar with Ralph's speaking may detect echoes of his voice from time to time in these pages. Of course any weaknesses or errors should not be traced to Ralph—that would not be reasonable or fair—but remain the author's responsibility.

Contents

SERIES INTRODUCTION

Living as a Christian

IN HUMAN TERMS, it is not easy to decide to follow Jesus Christ and to live our lives as Christians. Jesus requires that we surrender our selves to him, relinquish our aspirations for our lives, and submit our will to God. Men and women have never been able to do this easily; if we could, we wouldn't need a savior.

Once we accept the invitation and decide to follow Jesus, a new set of obstacles and problems assert themselves. We find that we are often ignorant about what God wants of us as his sons and daughters. For example, what does it mean practically to obey the first commandment—to love God with our whole mind, heart, and strength? How can we know God's will? How do we love people we don't like? How does being a Christian affect what we do with our time and money? What does it mean "to turn the other cheek?" In these areas—and many others—it is not easy to understand exactly what God wants.

Even when we do know what God wants, it can be quite difficult to apply his teaching to our daily lives. Questions abound. How do we find time to pray regularly? How do we repair a relationship with someone we have wronged or who has wronged us? How do we handle unruly emotional reactions? These are examples of perplexing questions about the application of Christian teaching to our daily lives.

Furthermore, we soon discover that Christians have enemies—the devil outside and the flesh within. Satan tempts us to sin; our inner urges welcome the temptation, and we find our will to resist steadily eroding.

Finally, we must overcome the world. We are trying to live in an environment that is hostile toward what Christians believe and how they live and friendly toward those who believe and do the opposite. The world in which we live works on our Christian resolve in many subtle ways. How much easier it is to think and act like those around us! How do we persevere?

There is a two-fold answer to these questions: To live successfully as Christians, we need both grace and wisdom. Both are freely available from the Lord to those who seek him.

As Christians we live by grace. The very life of God works in us as we try to understand God's teaching, apply it to our lives, and overcome the forces that would turn us aside from our chosen path. The grace we need is always there. The Lord is with us always, and the supply of his grace is inexhaustible.

Yet grace works with wisdom. Christians must *learn* a great deal about how to live according to

God's will. We must study God's word in scripture, listen to Christian teaching, and reflect on our own experience and the experience of others. Many Christians today lack this kind of wisdom. This is the need which the Living as a Christian series is designed to meet.

The book you are reading is part of a series of books intended to help Christians apply the teaching of scripture to their lives. The authors of Living as a Christian books are pastoral leaders who have given this teaching in programs of Christian formation in various Christian communities. The teaching has stood the test of time. It has already helped many people grow as faithful servants of the Lord. We decided it was time to make this teaching available in book form.

All the Living as a Christian books seek to meet the following criteria:

- **Biblical.** The teaching is rooted in scripture. The authors and editors maintain that scripture is the word of God, and that it ought to determine what Christians believe and how they live.

- **Practical.** The purpose of the series is to offer down-to-earth advice about living as a Christian.

- **Relevant.** The teaching is aimed at the needs we encounter in our daily lives—at home, in school, on the job, in our day-to-day relationships.

- **Brief and Readable.** We have designed the series for busy people from a wide variety of backgrounds. Each of the authors presents profound Christian truths as simply and clearly as possible, and illustrates those truths by examples drawn from personal experience.
- **Integrated.** The books in the series comprise a unified curriculum on Christian living. They do not present differing views, but rather they take a consistent approach.

The format of the series makes it suitable for both individual and group use. The books in Living as a Christian can be used in such group settings as Sunday school classes, adult education programs, prayer groups, classes for teen-agers, women's groups, and as a supplement to Bible study.

The Living as a Christian series is divided into several sets of books, each devoted to a different aspect of Christian living. This book, *Your Money and Your Life,* is part of a set of books which communicates essential Christian wisdom for maturing in Christ. To grow in living the Christian life, we must learn about such basic subjects as faith, love of God, love of neighbor, and our identity as sons and daughters of God. To reach spiritual maturity, Christians must know how God enables us to overcome the obstacles that inevitably arise: our own wrongdoing, the power of the world, the flesh, and the devil. *Your Money and Your Life* and other books in this set present practical, scripturally based teaching that will help you attain basic maturity in your Christian life.

The editors dedicate the Living as a Christian series to Christian men and women everywhere who have counted the cost and decided to follow Jesus Christ as his disciples.

Bert Ghezzi and Peter Williamson
General Editors

ONE

A Word about Money

MONEY. The word itself brings out the "ostrich" in many of us. In addition to normal anxieties about money—"Do I have enough? How can I get more?"—Christians are often plagued with additional concerns about whether they are handling their money properly. Add to this the growing concern over an increasingly unstable world economy, and the sand doesn't seem like such a bad place to stick one's head after all.

But Christians don't have to be confused, anxious, or discouraged about money. Why not, when the whole world is? Because we have God's word on the matter—an unfailing, authoritative, utterly reliable guide.

Jesus' teaching on money wasn't addressed to a class of graduate students interested in the influence of religious thought on economics. It was addressed to people who worried about money because money was important, who complained about their financial plight, and who probably argued with one another about money. Among the twelve apostles were fishermen operating a small family business under the constraint of heavy Roman taxation. They had families to provide for and to worry about. One of the apostles was a former tax collector; judging from others of his profession he had enjoyed the pleasures of wealth gained at the expense of his countrymen. He would have been what we sometimes call "money-smart"—he knew how to handle money and make it work for him. And he would have known from firsthand experience the power of money to lure a man's heart away from God and his ways. These were not the kind of men who would have been satisfied with pious platitudes; they were looking for God's word, and they listened to Jesus because they knew that he gave them the teaching of God.

Those first disciples, of course, didn't have to deal with the complexities of a worldwide economy. They didn't worry about balancing their checkbooks, and they weren't blessed or bothered by credit cards. They may have had more children to provide for, but, then again, they didn't have to pay for braces for their teeth.

Though they lived in a different economic era, the teaching they received was nonetheless God's word to mankind on money—as true in our complex economy as it was in a simple, stable agrarian economy; as true in times of plenty as in times of great need; true for inflation of varying digits and true for recessions, depressions, and periods of controlled economic growth. It was aimed at the rich, the poor, the middle class, the misers, the philanthropists; it was aimed at you and me. And just as it brought light and inner freedom to the early disciples, it brings light and freedom to us as well.

My aim in writing this book is not to provide detailed instructions about budgeting, financial planning, and the like. Others have already provided this information, and I don't have much to add about these important matters. Instead, I would like to present what Jesus and the New Testament writers taught about money.

I realize that many who are serious about being Christians are cautious about applying the teaching of scripture, afraid that it might require them to take an irresponsible approach to finances. What they have heard of the scriptural approach may have seemed too radical to be workable. I don't believe that this ought to be the case. The Christian teaching *is* radical inasmuch as it cuts without compromise to the spiritual heart of the matter. But it is not for daydreaming fanatics. After all, Jesus and his apostles were not naive; their aim was to set up a new society that could exist in the old order. And from the book of Acts and the New Testament letters, we can see that they accomplished their goal. They couldn't have done so with an unworkable, irresponsible approach to finances.

Just what is the Christian approach to money? The question is fraught with considerable controversy. One teacher tries to persuade us that God wants to raise our financial standard of living, while another with equal conviction urges us to pursue the path of poverty. Capitalists, socialists, and communists have all claimed to draw inspiration for their own economic systems from the biblical teaching on money. After hearing three or four mutually exclusive perspectives on one area of controversy after another—all of which seem to contain at least a grain of truth—some of us despair of knowing with clarity what the Christian's approach to money ought to be.

While there are some difficult questions about the Christian teaching on money, I am convinced that the main lines of the Christian approach are plain; I present this with the conviction and prayer that the teaching of the Spirit will, when applied personally, liberate us from anxiety over money and spiritual bondage to it, and that it will answer the most pressing concerns facing the person who wants his or her approach to finances to be the approach of a disciple of Jesus.

TWO

Jesus Is Lord

THE NEW TESTAMENT teaching about money begins with a simple, yet revolutionary assertion: Jesus is Lord. If we do not understand what the New Testament writers meant when they proclaimed, "Jesus is Lord," we can make no sense of what the Bible teaches about money.

To say that Jesus is Lord is not merely to affirm his divinity. It is not enough to simply acknowledge that he is God's Son; we need to make a personal commitment to follow him. It is not enough to pray to him as Lord; we need to obey him. It is not enough to have our sins forgiven by him; we need to do what he tells us.

When we acknowledge that Jesus is Lord, we acknowledge that he is in charge of everything—the cosmos, the creation, but more to the point, he is in charge of our life in all its aspects, including our money. If we want Jesus to be our Lord, we want to make every aspect of our life available to him, so that everything we are and everything we have is under his control.

Who's in Charge?

Jesus considered money one of the prime contenders for the mastery that he alone is meant to exercise. "No man can serve two masters," he observed. "He will either hate one and love the other or be attentive to one and despise the other. You cannot give yourself to God and money" (Mt 6:24). We should be realistic about how money can influence us. If we allow it, money can actually rule us.

The other day I was talking with an accountant about how he came to the point of making a serious Christian commitment. I asked him what his life was all about before he was Christian. His reply wasn't surprising. "Money. I wanted to make lots of it." He then went on to recount how money had taken charge of his life. After graduating from college, he devoted himself to becoming rich. He spent hours plotting and rehashing various schemes to make money. When his first financial venture met with frustration, he became anxious. The strain eventually gave way to a drinking problem, and before he knew it, his life was a mess.

Desire for wealth had obviously become the driving force in his life. Yet my friend observed that he never consciously decided to make money his chief aim in life. "I just assumed that money was what everyone wanted—everyone else seemed to be going after it, and I just fell in line with the crowd."

Money can have that effect on us. If we are not

careful, it can take charge of our lives. Rather than having our lives under the control of Jesus, our lives can be under the control of money. We can find ourselves thinking and worrying about money a great deal. When it is time to make an important decision, we find that the financial impact of the decision becomes the most important factor in our thinking. If a good job opportunity comes up in another city and promises financial improvement, we may decide to take it without ever asking what God thinks about it. We are happy when our financial fortunes look good, and depressed when they look bad. We find it difficult to do the right thing if we know that to do so will require financial sacrifice.

Of course, all this is not to say that money is bad, or that the followers of Christ should have nothing to do with it. Jesus himself did not shun the use of money. He didn't seem to have it in great quantities, but what he had, he used. From John's gospel, we learn that one of the disciples was charged with the duties of treasurer for the apostles. It was not beneath the dignity of Jesus or his disciples to have and use money.

But when it came to the question, "Who is in charge of a man's life?" Jesus left no doubt about whether money and God could exercise a co-regency. It was a simple matter of one or the other. If money is a person's first priority, then it is impossible to love and serve God. "No man can serve two masters. He will either hate one and love the other or be attentive to one and despise the other. You cannot give yourself to God and money."

Several years ago, I applied for a job as a counselor in a psychiatric center. The center was governed jointly by a hospital and another community agency. I had two separate interviews with two different people. During the interviews, I learned that both of the individuals would function as my boss. This struck me as a confusing arrangement. My suspicions were confirmed when both interviewers gave different answers when I asked what the job would entail. I turned the job down, knowing that I couldn't work for two different bosses, especially when the individuals had different ideas about what I ought to do with my time. The message to prospective disciples is clear: "You either serve God or money. If your first priority in life is money, then you cannot follow me."

Jesus knew that money posed problems for many people. Mark's gospel records an interview between Jesus and a young man.

> As he was setting out on his journey, a man ran up and knelt before him, and asked him, "Good Teacher, what must I do to inherit eternal life?" And Jesus said to him, "Why do you call me good? No one is good but God alone. You know the commandments: 'Do not kill, Do not commit adultery, Do not steal, Do not bear false witness, Do not defraud, Honor your father and mother.' " And he said to him,

> "Teacher, all these I have observed from my youth." And Jesus looking upon him loved him, and said to him, "You lack one thing; go, sell what you have, and give to the poor, and you will have treasure in heaven; and come, follow me." At that saying his countenance fell, and he went away sorrowful; for he had great possessions.
>
> And Jesus looked around and said to his disciples, "How hard it will be for those who have riches to enter the kingdom of God!"
>
> (Mk 10:17-23)

It is easy to stereotype the man whose God is money. We think of a money-hungry workaholic who has sold his soul to get rich; he would exploit his own grandmother to make a buck. Mark's account of the rich man's conversation with Jesus presents a very different picture. Here we have a man who, according to all the normal standards of the day, is a good fellow. He is a man who fears God and obeys God's law. When Jesus passes through his town on the way to Jerusalem, the man is attracted to his teaching. His question, "Teacher, what must I do to gain eternal life?" is another way of saying, "What do I have to do to become your disciple?" In other words, he is a decent man who is sincerely interested in becoming a disciple of Jesus.

As the interview between master and prospective disciple progresses, it looks as though the man might easily be added to those who follow Jesus.

He has obeyed the commands of God, yet realized that Jesus can offer him something that transcends mere obedience to the external demands of the law. Jesus clearly loves the man. However, when his spiritual eyes look into the man's heart, he sees that wealth has the dominant influence. Jesus invites the man to give up his wealth in order to follow him to Jerusalem. For the young man, this invitation represents his moment of decision. He is eager to be a disciple; yet he is reluctant to give up his wealth. In the end, wealth wins; the man went away grieving because he wanted to follow Jesus, but he wanted wealth more. In this case, he couldn't have both.

This account presents a warning to us. It is possible to prefer money to God, even though we are sincerely interested in following God and doing good. As much as we would like to have it otherwise, we cannot serve two masters.

The Love of Money

This warning is echoed in Paul's advice to Timothy: "But those who want to get rich fall into temptation and a snare and many foolish and harmful desires which plunge men into ruin and destruction. For the love of money is a root of all sorts of evil, and some by longing for it have wandered away from the faith, and have pierced themselves with many a pang" (1 Tm 6:9-10). This passage provides a good summary of the New

Testament warnings about money. Three aspects of the problem are stressed.

First, we are warned not to love money. Money is not presented as an intrinsic evil. The problem comes when we "*want* to get rich"; the problem comes from "longing for it." This is an important distinction. The wealthy are warned about the dangers of wealth because it invites an attachment which can compete with the lordship of Jesus. But the poor are not immune to the dangers of money simply because for them it is in short supply. It is possible to love money even if you don't have it. Fundamentally, it is not a question of what is in your wallet, but what is in your heart.

Second, the love of money introduces us to a constellation of other problems. Desire for wealth leads to "many foolish and harmful desires." The love of money is a root of "all sorts of evil." The love of money presents trouble enough when it prevents us from loving God first. But it also leads to a host of secondary troubles: anxiety, covetousness, interpersonal strife.

One of the more immediate evils that follows on the coattails of love for money is the loss of personal integrity, the willingness to compromise what shouldn't be compromised. Why do private abortion clinics proliferate? Partly because there is a tremendous amount of money to be made by performing abortions. Why would a magazine include an increasing number of pornographic photos in its pages? Because pornography makes money. Why would a Christian leader compromise his faith with phoney fund-raising schemes? The love of money is at the root of all sorts of evil.

Whenever we find ourselves tempted to compromise our standards for financial gain—whether through cheating on our income tax, lying about our age to get an insurance policy, or compromising ourselves in any number of ways small or large—we ought to consider whether or not love for money is fueling the temptation.

Third, eventually the love of money will destroy us. It will "plunge men into ruin and destruction." By longing for money, men and women have "wandered away from the faith, and have pierced themselves with many a pang." In other words, it can lead to drastic and potentially irreversible spiritual consequences. If nothing else, the instinct for self-preservation ought to inspire us to pause. Ironically, when we are motivated by love of money, we think that we are doing what is best for us; we think that we will derive great personal benefit by gaining wealth. But it is an illusion. What does it profit a man to gain the whole world and to lose his own soul in the process?

The New Testament urges us not to be naive about money. If we give ourselves over to the demands of money, if we place too high a priority on getting it and keeping it, if we desire it in a way that displaces our desire for God himself, then money can become a millstone tied around our necks, leading to our ruin. The issue must be settled decisively: Jesus alone is Lord, and everything else in life is subordinate to him. You cannot serve God and money.

THREE

Don't Worry

"MY HUSBAND AND I HAD been living comfortably on two modest incomes. Then I became pregnant. When we first thought of reducing the budget to fit one salary, pathetic scenes passed through my mind: going hungry, not having enough clothes for the baby, nothing under the tree at Christmas."

This woman describes a nearly universal experience: anxiety about money. Like love for money, anxiety about money is a potent spiritual influence that must be dealt with if we are to place our finances under Jesus' control. They are not isolated problems, of course, but work together to keep Christians in varying degrees of spiritual slavery to money. Anxiety about money can be a symptom of love for money. We tend to worry about the things that are highest on our list of priorities. If we love money, we will be more inclined to worry about it. Our insecurity and fearfulness about money may spur us to make it a more important part of our lives than would otherwise have been the case. Many sincere

Christians find themselves acting as if they love money, not because they truly desire it above God, but because they are anxious about it and their anxiety leads them to place a higher priority on it than they should.

I know a man whose family lost a great deal of money during the depression of the 1930s. His attitude of anxiety over money stems from his parents' reaction to that time of economic chaos. Years later, he is still engaged in a never-ending pursuit of money. No matter how large his bank account, he is never satisfied. He always thinks of an economic emergency for which he is not prepared. And his pursuit of wealth continues. His "love" for money—that is, his dedicated pursuit of accumulating money—has its roots in anxiety.

The letter of Hebrews speaks directly to this condition:

> Do not love money but be content with what you have, for God has said, "I will never desert you, nor will I forsake you!" Thus we may say with confidence: "The Lord is my helper, I will not be afraid; What can man do to me?"
>
> (Heb 13:5-6)

In other words, don't love money, don't invest your heart in it, don't make it the most important pursuit of your life, because the Lord is with you and he will help you. There is no need to love money when God is your helper.

Fear Inspires Anxiety

To understand the spiritual potency of anxiety over money, we should realize that it is linked with the most fundamental human fear: the fear of death. Does that surprise you? Remember that man is a fallen race. His pride, rebellion, and disobedience have severed his only tie with life: his relationship with God. As members of a fallen race, we are under the sentence of death. Death for each of us is a stark, inevitable reality. We were made from dirt—the basic elements of the earth—and through death we will return to dirt. Not a pleasant thought, but nonetheless it sums up our condition as part of the human race.

Understandably, the reality of death induces a fundamental fear in us. It lies behind many of the various fears from which we suffer. It lies behind the horror a small child experiences when he first catches sight of his own blood flowing from a scrape or minor cut. It lies behind the fear a wife experiences when her husband is late returning from work. The fear of death can fuel our anxiety for money, without us even realizing it: fear that we won't get enough food to keep us alive, fear that we won't have enough money to keep warm when the winter arrives. We can rely on money as a buffer to insulate us from the reality of danger—ultimately the danger of death.

When Jesus died and rose again, he dealt death a fatal blow. The author of the letter to the Hebrews wrote:

> Since the children have flesh and blood, he too [that is, Jesus] shared in their humanity so that by his death he might destroy him who holds the power of death—that is, the devil—and free those who all their lives were held in slavery by their fear of death. (Heb 2:14-15)

Now that we are reconciled to God in Jesus Christ, we can say, "O Death, where is your sting? O death where is your victory?" Because we are sons and daughters of God through faith in Jesus, things work differently for us. We are part of a new creation, a new society, a new kingdom. We have a heavenly Father who provides for our needs. Just as we have been liberated from the fear of death, we have been liberated from its corollary: anxiety over money.

Stop Worrying

> "Consider how the lilies grow. They do not labor or spin. Yet I tell you, not even Solomon in all his splendor was dressed like one of these. If that is how God clothes the grass of the field, which is here today, and tomorrow is thrown into the fire, how much more will he clothe you, O you of little faith! And do not set your heart on what you will eat or drink; do not worry about it. For the pagan world runs after all such things, and your Father knows that you need them. But seek his kingdom, and these things will be given to you as well." (Lk 12:27-31)

This passage is so familiar that we are tempted to skim over it as we would the poetic platitude on a greeting card. Instead, we should carefully consider what Jesus is saying.

First, Jesus is proposing a trade-off of responsibilities. Jesus was not the first rabbi to take on a group of disciples. It was common practice for a teacher in Israel to gather a number of disciples around him. But the relationship between the rabbi and his disciples was much different than the relationship between teachers and students that prevails in today's schools and universities. When a young man became a disciple, he left his father's authority and came under the authority of his teacher. And between the rabbis and their disciples, a certain "trade-off of responsibilities" took place. The disciple agreed to submit to his master and to serve the master's practical and personal needs. In return, the teacher took responsibility for instructing the disciples and in making sure that their needs were met. It was up to the disciples to cook, clean, and mend the rabbi's clothing, but it was up to the rabbi to make sure that all his disciples had enough food and clothing.

Of course Jesus was no ordinary rabbi. Unlike the teachers of his day, the teaching of Jesus was not derived from the authority of Moses, passed along from rabbi to rabbi. He was himself the truth, the word made flesh, the anointed king—both Son of David and Son of God. To become the disciple of such a rabbi was to come under the kingship of God himself. To serve him was to serve the kingdom of God.

To be Jesus' disciple meant—and means—that his Father takes responsibility for you. An ordinary rabbi, even with the best of intentions, might fail to provide for his disciples in difficult times. But not the Teacher who brought men into the direct care of the heavenly Father. "Your Father knows that you need such things. Seek out instead his kingship over you, and the rest will follow in turn." In other words, "concern yourself with being my disciple, and I will see that you are taken care of." That is the kind of relationship that Jesus offers to all who follow him.

Second, Jesus tells us to stop worrying. Because he has taken responsibility for us, the Lord directs us not to be anxious.

Jesus does not simply say, "You shouldn't be so anxious; you should have more faith." His words are more direct: stop worrying! God's intention is not the least bit veiled by these words, not the least bit complicated or difficult to interpret or understand. Perhaps other portions of the Bible are more puzzling, but this is not one of those passages.

Ordinarily the absolute necessity of food and clothing (the latter in certain climates, at least) make them objects of great concern. But there is one thing which is even more necessary than these for our well-being: the kingship of Jesus over us. So necessary is this one thing, that even compared with food and clothing we are to seek it first. If we find this one thing, everything necessary for our well-being will follow as a result. Choose to serve God; make it the desire of your life to know him, to be obedient to him, to see other men and women come to know him. The other things—the food, the drink, the clothing—will come.

Third, Jesus makes it clear that this teaching applies to disciples only. In Luke's account, the audience is carefully identified. Two groups are distinguished: a large crowd, numbering "many thousands," and a much smaller group of "disciples." In the first part of the chapter, the teaching is addressed to his disciples: "When a crowd of many thousands had gathered, . . . Jesus began to speak first to his disciples." Later, "someone in the crowd" presents a question, which Jesus answers, presumably addressing the whole crowd. Then the passage we have been considering begins, "Jesus said to his disciples, 'Therefore I tell you, do not worry . . .' "

The fact that his teaching is directed to his disciples rather than to the crowd at large is significant. These words were not intended for unbelievers, or for that matter, those who might be "lukewarm Christians"—people who identify themselves as Christians, but are not serious about following Christ. Jesus does not tell unbelievers to stop worrying. In fact, he says, "the unbelievers of this world are always running after these things," as if this is inevitable. Those who do not believe in Jesus have a good many things to worry about. Nor does he expect lukewarm Christians to be free from the anxiety that hounds them. It does little good to tell someone who does not know the fatherhood of God through a committed relationship with God's Son to stop being anxious. But to those who are serious about being disciples, Jesus does say, "stop worrying," with every expectation that his disciples can obey him.

Fourth, Jesus issues a direction, not a condemnation. Occasionally, Christians run aground on this passage. When they read Jesus' words about not being anxious, they feel condemned. The logic runs something like this: (1) disciples don't have to be anxious; (2) I am anxious and I can't seem to stop; (3) therefore I must not be a true disciple. This kind of thinking only adds fuel to anxiety. In addition to worrying about food and clothing, the person who thinks this way also worries about whether or not he or she is a true disciple. Since the promise of provision seems to apply to those who are disciples, these new doubts about one's status increase the original anxiety about food and clothing! I would suspect that more Christians have entertained such logic (or illogic) than are willing to admit it. Part of the difficulty comes from viewing this passage as providing criteria for who is and who is not a disciple. That is not what the passage is about. Instead, it is aimed at disciples who are anxious for various reasons. To them Jesus says, "Stop worrying. My Father will take care of your needs."

God Provides

One of the best ways to understand how we can be free from anxiety is to observe how God does provide for his disciples. A man I know by the name of Tim was convinced that God wanted him to stay in the area after he graduated from college, despite the fact that the employment prospects were bleak. Ours is a university town with plenty of educated people. Tim's college degree wasn't nearly as marketable as it might have been somewhere else. Tim spent a full year job-hunting, picking up a few odd jobs on the side. By the year's end he was still without a job, his net worth was $50, and his rent was due. (Housing costs in our town, by the way, have been among the highest in the nation.) At this point, Tim prayed that God would somehow provide the needed rent money—and soon! The next day, he found a check in his mailbox for the amount he needed to pay his rent. Interestingly, the check was not from a friend who knew of his need. It was a bonus check from one of Tim's previous employers—the first and, to his knowledge, the last bonus ever paid by this company.

FOUR

Work

IN LIGHT OF JESUS' second coming, some of the early Christians concluded that work was no longer necessary. Perhaps they compared themselves to the lilies, "which neither toil nor spin." At any rate, somewhere along the line, they missed the point. God does provide, and Jesus will come again, but he normally provides for us through productive labor, and before he returns we should not be idle.

St. Paul wrote to the church at Thessalonika:

> Keep away from every brother who is idle and does not live according to the teaching you received from us. For you yourselves know how you ought to follow our example. We were not idle when we were with you, nor did we eat anyone's food without paying for it. On the contrary, we worked night and day, laboring and toiling so that we would not be a burden to any of you. We did this, not because we do not have the right to such help, but in order to make ourselves a model for you to follow. For even when we were with you, we gave you this rule:

> "If a man will not work, he shall not eat."
> We hear that some among you are idle. They are not busy; they are busybodies. Such people we command and urge in the Lord Jesus Christ to settle down and earn the bread they eat.
> (2 Thes 3:6-12)

This echoes Paul's earlier instructions to "make it your ambition to lead a quiet life, to mind your own business and to work with your hands, just as we told you" (1 Thes 4:11).

Paul's answer to the problem of idleness is characteristically straightforward; if a man is not willing to work, don't give him anything to eat. Paul is not condemning the unemployed who want to work but cannot find jobs. Rather, he is speaking against idleness, the unwillingness to work for a living. Unemployed men and women whom I know have been anything but idle. In fact, they often work harder than when they held a regular job: looking for a job (in itself one of the most difficult jobs around), helping others with odd jobs, or volunteering time for Christian service. A man or woman in this position may well need financial help from his relatives, fellow church members, or the government. All these can be channels of God's provision. Paul's rule applies to those who are able to work but refuse, either because of irresponsibility or laziness or because of a phoney spirituality which presumes upon the provision of God.

Apparently, the problem wasn't restricted to

the church in Thessalonika. Consider the perspective Paul gave to Timothy. "If anyone does not provide for his own relatives, and especially for members of his immediate family, he has denied the faith and is worse than an unbeliever" (1 Tm 5:8). Those who fear that obedience to the biblical approach to finances will lead to financial irresponsibility should pay particular attention to these words of the apostle.

The account of creation in the book of Genesis gives us God's perspective on the role of work in our lives. First of all, it tells us that work is good. After God created Adam and placed him in the garden, he gave him work to do; he was given the responsibility to govern the garden as God's representative. Thus, work was not a result of the Fall; it was part of God's original plan. Work had a place in Paradise. After the curse which came with separation from God, work was destined to be difficult and frustrating. But the work given in the beginning was good.

Since Jesus came to restore God's original design for the human race, we can expect that God wants to bless our work. Apart from God, work was under a curse; now that we are reconciled to God, work comes under his blessing. Not all of the difficulties and frustrations are removed from work. These will remain until the redemption is completed at the return of Jesus, but the first installment of God's blessing is available now.

We can expect that it is normally part of God's plan to provide us with jobs that will meet our financial needs. I know of several instances where God intervened in a person's job search in an extraordinary way. One case I am aware of is so unusual that I hesitate to mention it. A dental student named Steve wanted to remain in town for the summer rather than return home where a lucrative summer job awaited him, because he wanted to capitalize on some unique opportunities for Christian growth and service. But he couldn't remain unless he found a job for the summer. After a fruitless job search, Steve knew that his time was running out. If he didn't get a job in the next day or two, he would have to leave. Whether out of sheer desperation or out of real faith, Steve decided to open the local telephone book randomly, set his finger down on the page, and dial the number. A research scientist at an environmental agency answered the phone, and Steve asked if the agency had any job openings. Just that day a research assistant had resigned and Steve's qualifications fit the job description. He was hired the next day. The point of this illustration is not to advance a particular job hunting method based on random selection of telephone numbers. (I've never tried it, advised someone to try it, or known anyone else but Steve who has tried it!) Instead, it shows us that the Christian looking for a job is not on his own. His father is looking out for him and will even work in the most unusual ways to provide for him.

In addition to helping us find jobs, the Lord will often provide promotions and raises when our needs increase. One man I know was working for the county government, receiving an adequate wage; it was adequate, that is, as long as his wife was also working. When it became necessary for his wife to stop working, he submitted a proposal to the agency to upgrade his position. Because of budgetary cutbacks in the county government, he was pessimistic about the success of his proposal. He was pleasantly surprised to hear that not only was the proposal accepted, but the salary increase was retroactive to the date he was hired. The week his wife stopped working, my friend received his retroactive pay.

As Christians band together to form closer, more highly committed relationships, a whole new avenue of God's provision opens up. Christians who know about job openings begin to tell their fellow Christians in need of a job. Those who need more training, but need encouragement and practical direction in order to receive that training, will find help as they discuss the matter with men and women who are committed to them. Personal problems that might sooner or later jeopardize a person's job will often surface in the context of committed personal relationships; these same Christian brothers and sisters can provide the kind of personal help that spills over into the work arena.

Sarah had lost a few administrative positions, in spite of the fact that she was a very competent administrator. An outsider might have been puzzled by her lack of success. But anyone who had close contact with Sarah over a period of time would have noticed her tendency to become moody and withdrawn. When some Christians who were close to Sarah noticed her moodiness, they were able to speak to her about it and make sure that she received help in overcoming the problem. As Sarah learned how to handle her mood swings better, she had more success in her job.

While we can expect God to provide for us when it comes to finding jobs and succeeding in them, our trust is not in the circumstances but in God himself. If a tidal wave should wash over our island, or the dollar, franc, or yen fail us, if the major industry in our town should go out of business, if an atomic bomb should fall on our little section of the globe, the words of Jesus still stand: Don't worry! God has promised to provide for our needs.

A young woman in our community married a Christian from an Asian country, who was studying in the United States. Debbie was raised in a family that was relatively prosperous. Though not wealthy herself, she found that God always provided for her—through her parents, and later, through the jobs that she had. When her husband returned to his homeland, Debbie went with him—a young American woman in a third-world nation encountering a way of life very foreign to her. Her husband's salary in the first years of their marriage wasn't enough to cover the family's basic needs.

With several days remaining before the next paycheck, Debbie looked in her cupboard and found the last remaining food in the house—a can of condensed milk. The sight of that single can of milk was too much for Debbie, and she burst into tears of self-pity. After a good cry, she prayed, "Lord, if I'm going to be here in this country to proclaim how good and great you are, I am going to need food. I need assurance that you will provide for me here. Provide us with enough food for the month in the next three days." Within the next three days the food arrived—through an unusual number of invitations to eat with neighbors and friends, through a man who dropped off a box of extra homegrown foods, through an anonymous gift. It wasn't the last time that she and her husband needed to pray for food near the end of the month, and it wasn't the last time that God provided for them in unusual ways when the usual means were inadequate.

Another example of God's provision happened closer to home. For the past two years, my part of the country has been hit by a severe economic recession; unemployment in one nearby city was twenty-five percent at the time of this writing. A friend of mine, Tom, who had earlier purchased a small house for his family, was first laid off from his job in television broadcasting. For the past year or so he has been without a stable job, but God has provided him with work and given him success in it. Tom landed a temporary job producing a television documentary under very trying circumstances. In spite of the obstacles, he produced a good film. When this job was completed, another opportunity opened up for him just in time. Again, he was able to work on another project with considerable success. When we sat down together and reflected on his experience over several months, the pattern of God's provision and blessing was evident. Even though Tom is still looking for a stable job, his financial needs have been met, he has been successful in the work he has done, and he is in a better position to find work now than when he was first laid off, due to the experience and personal contacts he has gained over the past year.

While resting in an easy chair after a day's work at a steady, well-paying job, it is difficult to imagine how God could provide for us if the normal means of his provision were removed. But he can. From the earliest times, God has revealed himself as One who can provide for his people when all the ordinary means are removed. When the people of Israel were marching through the wilderness on their way from Egypt to the land of Canaan, every normal means of sustenance was gone. They couldn't farm the land; they had no one to barter with; and the hunting in that region was poor. But God didn't restrict himself to the normal means. He sent quail to them in great numbers, and manna every morning. When their water supplies were exhausted, he caused water to flow out of a rock.

When Elijah, the prophet of Israel, declared a

period of draught, he was forced into hiding—and the draught affected his food supplies as well. But the God who announced the draught through Elijah provided ravens to bring him food—hardly a normal means of sustenance, but effective nonetheless.

FIVE

Enough

IF SOMEONE WERE TO OFFER to pay us for a particular service rendered, our first thought might be "Great! How much?" Once we understand God's intention to provide for us, we are likely to wonder just what he has in mind. Does his promise to provide mean that we can expect enough to tide us over when we are on the brink of starvation? Or does it mean that we can expect a luxurious expense account—nothing but the best?

Paul provides the essence of the New Testament answer to this question: "God can multiply his favors among you so that you may always have enough of everything and even a surplus for good works" (2 Cor 9:8). This passage does not present budgetary guidelines, but it does offer an important perspective on God's provision. Normally, the Lord wants us to have enough for our own needs and more than enough to help others. In the next chapters, we will consider these two aspects of God's provision, and what they were intended for.

Enough for What?

What did Paul have in mind when he said that God is able to provide us with "enough for everything"? While he doesn't specify in this passage, we get some idea from other things he wrote, particularly in his letter to Timothy.

> We brought nothing into this world, nor have we the power to take anything out. If we have food and clothing we have all that we need. Those who want to be rich are falling into temptation and a trap. They are letting themselves be captured by foolish and harmful desires which drag men down into ruin and destruction. (1 Tm 6:7-9)

"If we have food and clothing we have all that we need." If we have enough to meet our basic needs for food and clothing—for the necessities of life—we have enough and we should be content. Paul then warns against the desire for riches. "Watch out!" he says. "It is a trap. Consider what you need to live. Be content with that and watch out for the desire for more, because you can be captured by those desires. If you are, you may find yourself wanting more and more, much more than you need. That road ends in destruction."

If this desire for more was a trap in the time of Timothy, how much more is it a trap for us. We live in an age when the desire for more is greater perhaps than it has ever been. Consider some of the powerful factors that fuel this desire.

First, the increase of material goods has presented us with more things to desire. As a result of various technological breakthroughs which began over two hundred years ago, more material goods—products, gadgets, and machines—are available to people. There are simply more things that a person can desire than ever before.

Second, the rise of materialism has fueled our desire to possess the goods of this world. We have witnessed a large-scale abandonment of Judeo-Christian values, resulting in a spiritual void. This gap has been largely filled by a dependence on material things—not only for physical comfort—but for a sense of security, fulfillment, and happiness. In other words, people are desiring more not merely out of a natural desire for physical well-being; their desire for material things is further fueled by a spiritual restlessness.

Third, the expectation of "upward mobility" often makes people dissatisfied with life. Men and women of the past didn't expect their lot in life to improve with time. But most Americans today expect their financial and material level to improve with time. The young married couple expects to move from a rented apartment to a "starter home" (small and a bit run-down), then to "something a little more comfortable," with hopes of one day landing in that dream house. When economic conditions make this more difficult for a large number of people to realize, a great deal of frustration results.

Fourth, the influence of mass advertising increases our desires. We find ourselves the target of a massive campaign—which expends millions of dollars each year and relies on the latest discoveries concerning human behavior—to convince us that we don't have enough and that we *need* all sorts of things that human beings have never needed before. The normal "desires of the flesh," which are strong enough without outside support, are being pumped up to the bursting point through the influence of television, radio, and print advertising. As a result we suffer from a severe case of "inflated desires."

We all have our weak spots. The hamburger advertisements are hard on me. A sixty-second television commercial displaying one of those marvels in all its splendor makes eating my bologna sandwich seem like an exercise in asceticism. When I see that crisp lettuce, those fresh tomatoes, those perfectly placed pickles all piled high on a juicy patty of ground beef, I find that I want that hamburger. Who cares about the bologna sandwich sitting conveniently and inexpensively in the refrigerator!

Even minimum exposure to the advertising that bombards our society daily—a little television, a little radio in the car, a magazine or two each week, a few brochures in the mail, and the occasional billboard on the way to work—exposes us to a heavy dose of messages designed to increase our desire for a wide range of things. A trip to the Bahamas during the cold winter months, a food processor for the kitchen, a newer and better automobile, a retirement home in Arizona, a snowmobile, a home video system to take its place next to the color television and the personal computer, a variety of items to improve our appearance or health—the list is not easily exhausted.

As Christians living in a "desire-inflating" age, we need to let the word of God, which is "sharper than any two-edged sword" (Heb 4:12), cut us free from these influences. "We brought nothing into this world, nor have we the power to take anything out. If we have food and clothing we have all that we need. Those who want to be rich [to acquire more and more for themselves] are falling into a temptation and a trap. They are letting themselves be captured by foolish and harmful desires which drag men into ruin and destruction" (1 Tm 6:7-9). Rather than let our understanding of "enough" be shaped by society's definition, we should look to the Lord to find out what "enough" means for us.

This is not to imply that God's definition of "enough" is strictly limited to food and clothing, for every person in every circumstance. The New Testament does not propose one single lifestyle to which all Christians are held. Our actual needs vary. A businessman may need to spend more money on clothing than someone else if he is expected to dress according to certain standards in order to represent his firm. A person in one part of the world may need a car in order to do the things

God wants him to do, while someone in another environment may do well with a bicycle or public transportation.

What about the Future?

Trying to understand what "enough" means usually raises the question of providing for the future. Perhaps we feel that we have enough for the present, but we wonder whether we will have enough next year, or ten years from now. Concern for our future needs is increased when we consider our responsibility to provide for our children, for our parents, or for others for whom we are responsible.

If we look to the scripture to provide strict guidelines about whether, when, or how much money we should set aside for the future, we will be disappointed. Scripture does not spell out those guidelines. This is a matter in which we need to apply wisdom from God and the direction of the Holy Spirit to our particular situation. The most important teaching of the Bible on this matter can be summed up in this way: the main way the Lord wants us to provide for our future is to have Jesus as the effective Lord of our life. Everything is passing away; nothing is secure. The only thing that remains forever is God, his word, and his kingdom. In light of this, the best way to provide for the future is to be in the kind of relationship with God which allows him to lead, care for, and protect us. Compared with the security of having

God as our provider, every other form of provision for the future is risky. While it might be right for us to have money in the bank, or insurance policies of various kinds, we must realize that compared with the security that God provides his children, these things are not really safe at all.

The money in the bank may be practically worthless in ten years; the insurance companies may be out of business when we need them most. I know a man who worked for thirty years for a major city in the United States. During that time he invested in what seemed was a very secure retirement plan provided by the city. Twenty years prior to his retirement, the thought of a major American city going bankrupt seemed like science fiction; at the time he retired, the city was in dire financial straits and the retirement plan that had looked so secure was in potential danger.

A similar principle applies to providing for our children's future. Ordinarily, when we think of providing for the future of our children, we think of setting aside money for a college education, or establishing a trust fund. We may forget or at least underestimate the fact that the best way to provide for a child's future is to train him to work, to earn a living, and to know Jesus as his Lord. I've seen many children of affluent families corrupted because their parents did not provide these things, but instead provided more money for them than they should have. I know children raised by Christian parents who gave them all the money they wanted; these children abandoned the Lord largely because they were never taught basic discipline or the ability to deny themselves. This current runs deep in affluent cultures, where the tendency is to provide *too much* money but not nearly enough training in strong Christian character traits such as the ability to be patient, to work hard, to endure hardship, and to be trustworthy.

The fact that God is the only utterly reliable provision for our future needs does not mean that we should not own a life insurance policy, invest in a retirement fund, or save money for future needs. It does mean that we should only place our full confidence in God and not in sources which may fail us. When possible, some provision for future needs is reasonable.

The provident person is not the same as one who hoards for the future. The provident farmer, for example, is one who stores enough grain from this year's harvest to provide seed for next year's sowing. The rich farmer of the parable in Luke's gospel, on the other hand, was guilty of hoarding. After the great harvest he had one year, he tore down his barns to build bigger ones, intending to live a life of ease thereafter.

Personally, I think it wise to consider future needs and set aside money from present income to meet those needs. For example, you could probably predict with reasonable certainty how long your automobile will last. Rather than borrow money to buy another car when the old one gives out, you would be wise to set aside some money each month (perhaps for several years) to prepare for the inevitable. Similarly, you may prefer to send your children to a Christian school in spite of the increased expense. If this is the case, it is wise to begin to save for tuition as soon as your child is born so that the cost can be spread out over a longer period of time.

When possible, it is better to lower your present standard of living in order to provide for future needs than to live barely within your means with no concern for predictable future expenses.

Enough for the Body of Christ

We should view support for the body of Christians to whom we belong as part of our basic expenses, like food, clothing, or transportation. "The elders who direct the affairs of the church well are worthy of double honor, especially those who work is preaching and teaching. For the scripture says, 'Do not muzzle the ox while it is treading out the grain,' and, 'The worker deserves his wages'" (1 Tm 5:17-18). Similar instructions are found in the letter to the Galatians: "Anyone who receives instruction in the word must share all good things with his instructor" (Gal 6:6). The members of the Christian community are expected to support those who labor in the community as leaders and teachers.

The leaders of the first church in Jerusalem soon discovered that they needed to be freed from other duties in order to devote themselves to "prayer and the ministry of the word" (see Acts

6:2-4). Nearly every community needs people who have been relieved of other duties in order to pay more attention to prayer, teaching, and governing the community.

In addition, most churches, parishes, or fellowships have a variety of practical expenses (facilities for meetings, phone costs, and so on), as well as expenses for the mission of the group. Taken together, these expenses point to the need for substantial financial support by church members for the work of the church.

Many Christians have learned some important lessons about their financial responsibility in this area from an Old Testament practice called "tithing." The people of Israel were required by the law of Moses to give a tenth portion, also called a tithe, of "the seed of the land," "the fruit of the tree," and the "herd, or the flock" (see Lv 27:30-32). The tithe was given to the Levites, who were responsible for the administration and services of the tabernacle and, later, for the temple in Jerusalem. For convenience' sake, a monetary equivalent of the produce and livestock was given. In later years the commandment to tithe was elaborated by burdensome interpretations of the law, which led to an unhealthy preoccupation with tithing even on such things as "mint, dill, and cummin." It was this detailed and burdensome approach to tithing that Jesus criticized when he said to the Pharisees, "Woe to you, scribes and Pharisees, hypocrites! For you tithe mint and dill and cummin, and have neglected the weightier provisions of the law: justice and mercy and faithfulness; but these are the things you should have done without neglecting the others" (Mt 23:23).

Originally, the Old Testament tithe was not a petty religious practice but one of the means by which the people of God took responsibility for the worship of God in the temple. The tithe expressed thanksgiving for God's provision and reminded the people that everything they had came from God and belonged to him. The giving of the tithe brought honor to God: "Honor the Lord with your wealth, with first fruits of all your produce" (Prv 3:9).

To neglect the practice of tithing was considered "robbing God." "Will a man rob God? Yet you rob me. But you ask, 'How do we rob you?' In tithes and offerings!" (Mal 3:8).

The concept of the Old Testament tithe can serve as a useful guideline for meeting our financial responsibility for the work of the body of Christ. If the people of the old covenant provided a tenth of their produce and livestock to support the temple services, it seems reasonable for Christians to contribute ten percent of their income to meet the needs of the body of Christ. Many Christian groups have agreed together to support their fellowship by having each of the members contribute ten percent of their income.

Our financial support may be expressed by contributions to a single congregation, but it is not always as simple as that. Some people may be part of a church congregation or parish which allows for only a limited expression of membership. To supplement their church membership, they may be active in another form of Christian fellowship. They might contribute some portion of their tithe to each group, or send a portion to another ministry which strengthens the broader body of Christ in some particular way. It is even possible that a person might belong to a church which is spending its money on efforts which he or she cannot wholeheartedly support. It would be reasonable to contribute less to such a church in order to channel the money in another direction.

Perhaps the most helpful lesson to be learned from the Old Testament practice of tithing is that tithing was viewed as a "family responsibility." The Israelite in the time of the old covenant tithed because he was part of the people of God; as a result he bore responsibility for the administration of the temple. Paying the tithe was not like giving alms from the surplus God had given him; it was like providing food and clothing for his family—a responsibility, not an act of charity.

Too often, Christians think of their tithe as a "charitable contribution," like giving to the cancer society. It is nothing of the sort. This is not a "good work" any more than providing for our families is. Because we are part of this people—the people of God—we are responsible for the needs of the family.

A friend named Gary was running into some financial trouble. He had a wife and a new child, and only $300 from his last paycheck, and he didn't know where his next check would come from. As soon as he cashed the check he sent $30 to the Christian community to which he belonged. He didn't think of this as irresponsible or as an act of extraordinary generosity in the face of personal need.

Gary had a good attitude. He considered his contribution to the body of Christians to which he belonged as a part of the "enough" that God provides us, rather than as part of the "surplus for good works." When we consider how much money to spend as part of our regular necessary expenditures, our financial responsibility to the Christian group to which we belong.

A relatively new Christian once came to me and said, "Do I need to give ten percent of my *gross* or *net* income?" He was thinking of his contribution as if it were his dues for membership in the Kiwanis Club. "How much do I need to pay to belong?"

The words of an evangelical scholar, F.F. Bruce, would have provided an apt response: "He [the Christian] should not ask, 'What am I required to give?' but 'How much can I give?' and then 'How much more can I give?' " (F.F. Bruce, *Questions and Answers* [Grand Rapids, Mich.: Zondervan, 1972), p. 244.]

SIX

More than Enough

BEYOND PROVIDING "enough for everything," God wants to provide us with a surplus. He wants to give us more than we actually need. But note carefully what this surplus is for: "God can multiply his favor among you so that you may always have enough of everything and even a surplus *for good works*" (2 Cor 9:8).

Christians are easily confused when it comes to understanding the purpose of the surplus God wants to give us. At one extreme, we can get the impression that the truly "spiritual" Christian should only make enough money to meet his or her basic needs. Lucrative jobs, promotions, financial blessings are considered temptations to be avoided. At the other extreme, financial blessing is viewed as an end in itself—as if the really faithful Christians are the ones who are "blessed" with a luxurious lifestyle. Both perspectives miss the mark. The Lord does not normally want us to avoid having a financial surplus; he wants to give us more than we actually need. But the reason he provides the surplus is not so that we can raise our standard of living, but so that we can have enough for good works.

Jesus told a story about a man who was guilty of misusing his abundance.

> The land of a certain rich man was very productive. And he began reasoning to himself, saying, "What shall I do, since I have no place to store my crops?"
>
> And he said, "This is what I will do: I will tear down my barns and build larger ones, and there I will store all my grain and my goods. And I will say to my soul, 'Soul, you have many goods laid up for many years to come; take your ease, eat, drink, and be merry.' " But God said to him, "You fool! This very night your soul is required of you; and now who will own what you have prepared?"
>
> So is the man who lays up treasure for himself, and is not rich toward God.
>
> (Lk 12:16-21)

The man wasn't faulted for having an abundant harvest; we can assume that his especially fruitful crop was a blessing from God. Rather, it was his "reasoning" that got him into trouble. Though he already had enough to fill his barns, he decided to build bigger barns—enough to allow him to take it easy for years to come. He went beyond a reasonable provision for the future and hoarded his surplus. He didn't use his God-given surplus for its God-given purpose. If he had done that, he would have been "rich toward God"; instead, he laid up treasure for himself and was forced to answer for his misuse of God's provision.

This story stands as a warning to us. It is evident that the Lord is not pleased with the man or woman who builds bigger barns to store up the surplus; he has different designs on that money. One of the questions we will be asked when we meet the Lord is, "What did you do with the extra resources I put into your hands?"

Almsgiving

Almsgiving is clearly the main channel through which to direct our surplus. Almsgiving is something that Jesus expects his disciples to do. His teaching on giving alms begins, "*when* you give alms," as if the question, "*should* we give alms," is not even worth asking.

The context for most of the New Testament teaching on almsgiving concerns providing for Christians who are poor. For example, Paul's teaching to the Corinthians concerns a collection for the poor in the Jerusalem church. This reflects the fact that our relationship with fellow Christians is a family relationship. Just as we have a greater responsibility to provide for the members of our family than we have to provide for others (as Paul says, "the man who does not care for his own relatives is worse than an unbeliever"), our giving to the poor ought to begin with poor believers.

However, this does not mean that we are to restrict our almsgiving to poor Christians. Jesus taught:

> If you love those who love you, what credit is that to you? Are not the tax collectors doing that? And if you greet only your brothers, what are you doing more than others? Do not even pagans do that? But be perfect, even as your father in heaven is perfect. (Mt 5:46-47)

By this Jesus is not saying that we should neglect giving alms to poor fellow Christians. He is saying that if we are to be like our heavenly Father, we can not restrict our love to those who love us in return.

As usual, the teaching of Jesus humbles us before it exalts us. Just when we begin to think that we are doing something extraordinary, we learn that we are only doing our duty.

In addition to providing for the poor, our surplus is also intended to be used to support various projects which could truthfully be called "God's work." This would include works which advance the kingdom of God—efforts to preach the gospel to all the peoples of the earth, efforts to establish Christian communities where there are none, efforts to translate the scriptures into the many languages which have no translations of the Bible, and efforts to renew or restore the body of

Christ where it is weak, divided, or losing sight of its moorings. We are living in a time of unprecedented opportunity to engage in fruitful work for the sake of God's kingdom. It is a time of great spiritual conflict when "all hands are needed on deck," when all the available resources of God's people can be put to use. In many places around the world the spiritual harvest is ripe, but much is left undone because funds are not available to send Christian workers. One of the main reasons for the lack of funds is that many of us are not apportioning our surplus as well as we might. Whether our surplus is great or small, we ought to be looking for ways to support God's work.

Part of supporting God's work includes providing financial backing for some of God's servants—men and women who are called to serve in a particular mission. Charles Finney, a noted nineteenth-century evangelist, tells in his memoirs of a man who gave him $600 year after year so that he could continue his preaching in the Northeastern United States. During those years, Finney spearheaded a spiritual awakening which directly affected the lives of hundreds of thousands of people and strengthened the movement to abolish slavery in the United States. The $600 which supported Finney during a year was money well spent.

This practice of providing for the Lord's servants so that they can be engaged in the Lord's work can be traced back to the New Testament itself, which records the Philippians' support of the apostle Paul (see Phil 4:16), well as the women who provided for Jesus and his disciples "out of their means" (see Lk 8:2-3).

It ought to be a source of grief for us all that a number of organizations within Christian churches which at one time advanced worthwhile causes do so no longer. They have gotten off track for one reason or another. If a Christian organization isn't advancing the cause of Christ, we shouldn't support it financially—even if the organization has a long and venerable history of good works.

How to Give

While the New Testament teaching on money places great importance on giving, it places an equal importance on the manner in which we give. In particular it teaches us to give without ostentation, and to give willingly, not begrudgingly.

Don't blow your horn. "When therefore you give alms, do not sound a trumpet before you, as the hypocrites do in the synagogues and in the streets, that they may be honored by men. Truly I say to you, they have their reward in full. But when you give alms, do not let your left hand know what your right hand is doing that your alms may be in secret; and your Father who sees in secret will repay you" (Mt 6:2-4).

Giving alms is something we ought to do out of love for and obedience to God. "He who is kind to the poor lends to the Lord, and he will repay him for his deed" (Prv 19:17). If we give alms in order to draw the attention of men, we will not draw the attention or receive the reward of God. Therefore we are urged to give alms in secret, so that only God knows what we have done.

Don't clench your teeth. "Let each do just as he has purposed in his heart; not grudgingly or under compulsion; for God loves a cheerful giver" (2 Cor 9:7). When Paul appealed to the Corinthians for funds to be sent to the church in Jerusalem, he was not interested in extracting as much money as he could. He knew that God wanted a gift freely given from eager hearts. So he warned the believers not to give out of compulsion—because they had been pressured into giving against their will—but to give whatever they could decide to give freely and generously; no more and no less.

This is not to say that we should only give what we can easily give, without "wincing," without experiencing a tug toward selfishness. Because we struggle against an inward inclination not to do the will of God, we cannot wait until all of our second thoughts about giving have vanished before contributing. We can decide to do what we know the Lord wants even though we may have conflicting desires; and once we have decided to give, we should do it without grumbling. A husband once complained to me that his wife had forced him into a decision to take a job he didn't like. Actually, his wife had simply persuaded him to take the job. I pointed this out to him and reminded him that he wasn't really forced into anything. It was his decision to make and he made it. Once we make voluntary decisions, we should not carry them out as if forced to, like a slave grudgingly carrying out the will of his master.

Regular Review. In addition to the biblical directives about giving, I would add a practical suggestion. That is, that you *regularly* consider giving alms or financial support for the Lord's work as part of the way you manage your finances. I have found that it is all too easy to forget about giving, or to wait for a compelling desire to give. The result is that I am not as generous as I might be. It isn't necessary to set aside a regular amount each month to be allotted to alms much as you would allot a certain amount to the water bill (though this might be a good thing to do), but that you regularly consider whether, how much, and to whom you ought to be giving money; this is something you can do along with monthly financial chores like balancing the checkbook, but do it prayerfully, with an openness to the Holy Spirit giving some direction and inspiration.

SEVEN

Advice to the Rich

THE NEW TESTAMENT does not outlaw riches. Jesus forbids riches or anything else, for that matter, which takes precedence over following him, but the state of being rich is neither commended as a sign of God's favor nor condemned as a sign of sinful greed. The New Testament does, however, warn the rich of the dangers of wealth, and it does urge the wealthy to freely give money away. In short, everyone should give, but the rich should give more.

> Command those who are rich in this present world not to be arrogant nor to put their hope in wealth, which is so uncertain, but to put their hope in God, who richly provides us with everything for our enjoyment. Command them to do good, to be rich in good deeds, and to be generous and willing to share. In this way they will lay up treasure for themselves as a firm foundation for the coming age, so that they may take hold of the life that is truly life.
>
> (1 Tm 6:17-19)

We should begin by remembering that "the rich" here referred to may not be just the luxuriantly wealthy. In the same chapter of Paul's letter to Timothy, Paul says, "If we have enough for food and clothing, we have all that we need. Those who want to be rich . . ." (1 Tm 6:7). By implication, anyone who has more than they need to live is relatively rich. This advice could apply, then, to almost everyone who reads this book. Perhaps we are only "a little rich," but rich, nonetheless, according to Paul's standard of wealth.

To those of us with more than enough to meet our basic needs, the Lord provides some sound financial advice. We ought to invest our money while there is still time to gain a heavenly return on our investment. We need to exchange the wealth of this age for the wealth of the age to come. In doing so, we are not achieving an extraordinary level of generosity; we are simply being smart with our money.

Jesus told a story about a shrewd manager who learned that he was soon to be fired by his master. In order to gain the friendship of his master's debtors, he called them in one at a time and forgave portions of their debt. This manager was commended, not for his dishonesty, but for his shrewdness. "The master commended the dishonest manager because he had acted shrewdly. For the people of this world are more shrewd in dealing with their own kind than are the people of the light. I tell you, use worldly wealth to gain friends for yourselves, so that when it is gone, you will be welcomed into eternal dwellings" (Lk 16:8-9).

The Lord is urging us to be every bit as shrewd as the dishonest manager in our use of wealth. Looking into the financial prospects for the future is a key element in the wise use of our money.

If, for example, we knew that the world would soon be dominated by the Republic of China, we would be smart to exchange our American dollars, English pounds, German marks, Russian rubles, or Mexican pesos into yuan, the Chinese currency. We would be foolish to hold on to depreciating currency rather than exchanging it for currency with a brighter financial future.

In fact, we do know about an even more radical shift in the present world order than would occur if China should become the ruling world power. We know that this entire age will come to an end; our participation in it will come to an end when we die, and at some point the age itself will end for everyone. In its place will come a new order, with a new economic base and a new currency. This new order will be the kingdom of God, fully established by the second advent of Christ. If we know that this age will be ending relatively soon, or that our participation in it will be ending within a mere ten, twenty, thirty, or sixty years, we would be foolish not to let this knowledge play a major role in our investment strategy.

If we are smart, we will take Paul's advice to "do good, to be rich in good works and generous, sharing what [you] have. Thus [you] will build a secure foundation for the future, for receiving the life which is life indeed."

This is precisely the advice that too many of us fail to take seriously. Ironically, many who are stingy with their wealth think that they are avoiding a naive generosity in order to be shrewd in their money management. I have an acquaintance who is relatively wealthy, and quite generous as well. When some members of his family notice his generosity, they upbraid his irresponsibility. In fact, this man is simply a shrewd investor. He is investing his wealth in something that will bring a certain return at an extraordinarily high yield.

In the story of the wealthy man and Lazarus, we see the tragic results of not investing our money with the age to come in mind.

> There was a rich man who was dressed in purple and fine linen and lived in luxury every day. At his gate was laid a beggar named Lazarus, covered with sores and longing to eat what fell from the rich man's table. Even the dogs came and licked his sores.
>
> The time came when the beggar died and the angels carried him to Abraham's side. The rich man also died and was buried. In hell, where he was in torment, he looked up and saw Abraham far away, with Lazarus by his side. So he called to him, "Father Abraham, have pity on me and send Lazarus to dip the tip of his finger in water

> and cool my tongue, because I am in agony in this fire."
>
> But Abraham replied, "Son, remember that in your lifetime you received your good things, while Lazarus received bad things, but now he is comforted here and you are in agony. And besides all this, between us and you a great chasm has been fixed, so that those who want to go from here to you cannot, nor can anyone cross over from there to us." (Lk 16:19-26)

The rich man had every opportunity to use his "worldly wealth to gain friends." Lazarus could have become one of these friends through the rich man's generosity; if the rich man had capitalized on these opportunities, he might have been "welcomed into eternal dwellings" by his friend Lazarus. Instead, he let personal greed cloud his good judgment, and he failed to act shrewdly, to invest his wealth wisely. His fate acts as a warning to all of us to make good use of the money we have, making sure that we are "rich in good works and generous, sharing what we have" with those who can someday welcome us in the age to come.

Of course, this is a warning and an encouragement to us only if we are convinced that this present age *will* come to an end, and that our conduct in this life will have lasting consequences for the next. Among major sectors of the Christian church this perspective—the transitory nature of this age, the certainty of its impending end, the reality of heaven and hell—has been largely forgotten, or swept under the rug with other embarrassingly supernatural Christian teachings. Yet in these same sectors of Christianity, we see renewed emphasis on the obligation of the rich to care for the poor. Without an understanding of the motivation for generosity presented in the New Testament, this emphasis is not likely to produce lasting results. Jesus' reading of human nature was right. Left to our own devices, we are short-sighted; if we look into the future at all, we do not look deeply enough to penetrate the veil that separates this life from the life to come. In order to follow his teachings, we must embrace the eternal perspective that is central to his teaching. In order to use money as a Christian, we have to understand that the Christian's financial principles are rooted in an eternal, rather than a merely temporal, perspective.

The Principle of Equality

Many people are afraid to be generous with their money lest they become poor. What good am I to my family or to other needy people if I become too poor to do anything but feed and clothe myself? Paul addresses this problem by presenting the principle of equality as a guideline for our giving.

> I am about to give you some advice on this matter of rich and poor. It will help you who

began this good work last year, not only to carry it through, but to do so willingly. Carry it through now to a successful completion, so that your ready resolve may be matched by giving according to your means. *The willingness to give should accord with one's means, not go beyond them. The relief of others ought not to impoverish you; there should be a certain equality.* Your plenty at the present time should supply their need so that their surplus may one day supply your need, with equality as the result. It is written, "He who gathered much had no excess and he who gathered little had no lack."

(2 Cor 8:10-15)

"The relief of others ought not to impoverish you." Ordinarily, the Lord does not ask us to become poor in the process of helping those who have less than we do. "The willingness to give should accord with one's means, not go beyond them." The way is open for the widow who was commended by Jesus because she "gave from her want, all that she had to live on," to the temple treasury. The way is also open for the rich young man to sell all that he has, give alms, and follow Jesus. The way is open for men and women to follow the example of Francis of Assisi and others like him, who dedicated himself to the Lord through a commitment to poverty. But normally the relief of others should come from our plenty.

"There should be a certain equality." Paul, who was giving the Corinthians guidelines for their

contribution to the poor of the Jerusalem church, lays down the principle that "there should be a certain equality" between the two churches. When one group has an excess and the other has a lack, those with more should provide for those with less, "with equality as the result."

It is helpful to consider the source from which Paul derived this principle of equality. It is an Old Testament source, a passage from the book of Exodus: "He who gathered much had no excess, and he who gathered little had no lack" (Ex 16:18). This passage refers to God's provision of manna for the Israelites during their wilderness journey from Egypt to the Promised Land.

The wilderness journey represented a special time in the history of the chosen people. It was a time when God was especially close to them. He led the Israelites by the pillar of fire and the cloud which hovered over them. He provided food from heaven and water from a rock when they had no normal means for satisfying their hunger and quenching their thirst. It was a time when all of the people were taken care of. Each person had enough.

Paul applied this Old Testament passage to the Corinthian Christians, who had become members of the people of God—the people of the New Covenant, who had been delivered from bondage to sin and were making their way to the promised land of everlasting life. Among the people of the New Covenant, just as among the people of Israel during the wilderness journey a "certain equality should prevail." The one who gathers much of God's provision should have no excess, because he gives it to the one who gathers little.

Though the Corinthian Christians were a predominantly Gentile congregation and the Jerusalem Christians were a predominantly Jewish congregation, Paul wanted the Corinthians to see that the Jewish believers were their brothers. Even though the two churches were located in different regions of the empire, living in relative isolation from each other, Paul wanted them to understand that they were part of the same people. Like the Israelites making their way through the desert to the land of Canaan, the Christians from Corinth and Jerusalem were "in this thing together." Because they were part of the same people, the same family, they bore a financial responsibility for each other.

The equality that Paul urged the Corinthians to aim for is not the kind of equality in which everyone dresses the same, has the same amount of money, and drives the same kind of car. He was concerned that everyone's needs be met. The brother with an excess should eagerly provide for the brother in need. As part of one family, the Christians should be looking out for each other.

How do we apply this teaching in our own lives? It raises some complicated questions. With the churches divided and in a state of general confusion, it is difficult to know precisely who and where the Christians are. How can a Christian in London share from his excess with a fellow Christian in Singapore?

These complex questions are clearly beyond the scope of this book. But there are some things that we ought to do, even before we know the answers to these tough questions. First, we should consider the Christians we know. Are they being taken care of? Do they have enough? Or are they suffering financial lack that our plenty can alleviate? Even here, we have to operate by good wisdom. If a Christian in your church abuses his credit cards, buys a roomful of new furniture on credit, then finds himself in a financial bind, perhaps he should face at least some of the consequences of financial irresponsibility rather than have someone bail him out.

We can gain the wisdom that we need to balance important considerations like these, but the wisdom is useless without the willingness among Christians to share their resources with the people they know. If we can't apply Paul's teaching to the brother we can see, we waste our time looking for answers to worldwide economic problems. Our first thought, then, ought to be for the people in our weekly Bible study or prayer group, those in our local congregations and parishes, the Christians we know.

In the past few years, I have noticed more sharing of financial resources among the Christians I am familiar with. A family which is outgrowing its rented apartment is in need of a house, but doesn't have the money for a down payment. A single man who is a lawyer wins a lucrative case and offers the proceeds to help the family out. A group of college students work and live together during the summer. One of the women earns less money than expected so the others chip in to help meet her expenses.

Having learned to share our resources with those we know, we can apply these same lessons to Christians in other places. Though tough questions face us once we think of sharing on a cross-national level, we still have some responsibility. How we exercise this responsibility will depend on the particular church we belong to and the means for sharing available to us. I know a Catholic woman who collects supplies for the needy in Poland. An evangelical Protestant friend of mine contributes money to an organization which distributes money on an international level. Another sends money to an elderly Pentecostal woman in India who provides for poor children in her area. If we are looking for good ways to share our excess, we will find them.

EIGHT

The Generosity Gift

I KNOW A MAN with a special knack for making money. He has a talent for increasing the money he has by making good investments and by exercising wise management. In fact, money seems to come to him from several directions at once. He gets more salary increases than anyone I know. He finds an old childhood coin collection, which is now worth thousands of dollars. He keeps careful records of his expenses and is able to save considerable money on his tax returns. He is always finding "good deals." But not only does he have a talent for making money, he has a talent for giving it. Those who know him well also know that he is often the first to offer money to someone in need. Though his income is increasing, he tries to keep his budget from increasing too, so that more of his money is available for needs other than his own.

I think this person has a special gift, a spiritual gift, for bringing in and giving money. I suspect that there are many others who have this same gift without realizing it.

> For just as we have many members in one body and all the members do not have the same function, so we, who are many, are one body in Christ, and individually members of one another. And since we have gifts that differ according to the grace given us, let each exercise them accordingly: if prophecy, according to the proportion of faith; if service, in his serving; or he who teaches, in his teaching, or he who exhorts, in his exhortation; *he who gives, with liberality*; he who leads, with diligence; he who shows mercy, with cheerfulness. (Rom 12:4-8)

When we speak of spiritual gifts, this gift of generosity is often neglected. It is much easier to recognize a prophetic gift, or a teaching gift, or a gift for healing. What is this gift, and how does it operate?

First of all, to say that some members of the body of Christ have a special gift for generous giving does not mean that a few people have a corner on the market. Generosity is part of the new nature that we take on when we live "in Christ." It is for all of us, not just a select group of specially gifted individuals.

However, while generosity is a trait that should characterize every Christian, I believe that God does give a special gift for giving to some members of the body. The same could be said of other gifts. Some Christians are called to a special teaching ministry (one that James says not many should seek), but this does not mean that most every

Christian should not teach. Fathers, for example, are responsible to teach their families, though only some fathers have a special gift for teaching. All mothers are responsible for teaching their children, regardless of whether they have a special gift. The same could be said for the ministry of showing mercy. For instance, one order of single women in the Roman Catholic Church devotes itself to the care of incurably ill cancer patients. They are called the Hawthornites, after their foundress, Rose Hawthorne. Many of them have worked twelve hours a day, seven days a week, for several years. They have a special ministry for showing mercy. Yet all of us are to show mercy, whether or not we have a special gift for showing mercy as others have. That is how it works with the gift of generous giving—all of us are to be generous, while some of us are called to a particular ministry of generosity, for which we are given a special gift for giving.

George Mueller, a German Christian who lived in England during the nineteenth century, was a man who seemed to have a special gift for bringing in and distributing money for the Lord's work. Mueller organized care for orphans in London—a particularly pressing need at that time. He was a man of deep faith and vigorous prayer. In fact, prayer was his chief means for raising money for his orphanages. It is estimated that during a ten-year period, Mueller received £26,000 and gave £22,330 of this for the care of orphans and for other Christian work.

A few years ago I had a conversation with a young man who had recently graduated from college. I asked him if he had any indication of what gifts he had to serve the Lord. He paused for a moment, then replied, "I think God has given me an ability to make a lot of money in order to contribute it to his work." This impressed me. And most men or women in his position would be eager to earn a great deal of money—but for themselves, not the Lord's work. And most young Christians in his position who are eager to serve God in a significant way automatically think of becoming a pastor, teacher, or leader. But this young man had a broader vision of Christian service, one that valued the gift of generous giving.

Conclusion

THOSE WHO HANDLE MONEY God's way will be rewarded. Some of us may think it beneath our dignity to be motivated by the prospect of rewards. We ought to do what is right, whether or not a reward is involved. True enough. But I think that we can use all the motivation we can get to follow the Lord, to do things his way, rather than our own way. If we are reluctant to let the prospect of rewards motivate us, perhaps our sense of dignity is a bit false. The Lord himself certainly doesn't seem to hide the fact that those who do things his way will be rewarded. Consider the rewards connected with the way we handle money:

> Honor the Lord with your wealth, with the firstfruits of all your crops; Then your barns will be filled to overflowing, and your vats will brim over with new wine. (Prv 3:9-10)

> "Bring the whole tithe into the storehouse, that there may be food in my house. Test me in this," says the Lord Almighty, "and see if I will not throw open the floodgates of heaven and pour out so much blessing that you will not have room enough for it. I will prevent pests from devouring your crops, and the vines in your fields will not cast their fruit," says the Lord

> Almighty. "Then all the nations will call you blessed, for yours will be a delightful land," says the Lord Almighty. (Mal 3:10-12)
>
> Do not be afraid, little flock, for your Father has been pleased to give you the kingdom. Sell your possessions and give to the poor. Provide purses for yourselves that will not wear out, a treasure in heaven that will not be exhausted, where no thief comes near and no moth destroys. (Lk 12:32-33)
>
> Give, and it will be given to you. A good measure, pressed down, shaken together and running over, will be poured into your lap. For with the measure you use, it will be measured to you. (Lk 6:38)

We can expect to receive three different rewards for believing and obeying the Lord's teaching about money.

The built-in rewards. Some rewards are built in to the very act of obedience. If we rely on the Lord as our provider, we are rewarded with a freedom from anxiety over money. If we obey his commands concerning money, we enjoy the reward of a clear conscience.

The future rewards. If we are generous with our riches in this life, we will receive greater riches in the life which is to come. These are the imperishable riches which cannot be taken from us, which cannot depreciate or wear out; they are the riches

KEN WILSON

AUTHOR

YOUR MONEY AND YOUR LIFE

TITLE

DATE LOANED	BORROWER'S NAME	DATE RETURNED

DATE LOANED	BORROWER'S NAME	DATE RETURNED

that we can enjoy, not for a few brief decades, but for eternity.

The present reward. If our rewards were restricted to peace of mind and our future inheritance in the coming kingdom of God, that would be enough. But there is no indication that God will not also reward us in this life, or that he will not reward us with material things. And there is plenty of positive evidence to the contrary.

> "I tell you the truth," Jesus replied, "no one who has left home or brothers or sisters or mother or father or children or fields for me and the gospel will fail to receive a hundred times as much in this present age (homes, brothers, sisters, mothers, children and fields—and with them, persecutions) and in the age to come, eternal life." (Mk 10:29-30)

Certainly Jesus is not saying that the present rewards are the most important ones, or that the present rewards are marks of a true disciple; but the present, material rewards associated with being a disciple are undeniably included.

We can expect to be rewarded with material things when we demonstrate that we can be trusted to handle material resources according to the design of the provider.

> Give, and it will be given to you . . . For with the measure you use, it will be measured to you . . .

> to him who has will more be given . . . whoever can be trusted with very little can also be trusted with much . . . if you have not been trustworthy with someone else's property, who will give you property of your own? (Lk 6:38; 16:10, 12)

Rather than shun or underestimate the rewards that come with believing and obeying God's word about money, we should let the prospect of rewards motivate us to hear and live by God's word. Years ago, Christians not only accepted the fact that obedience to God would be rewarded (and disobedience punished), they meditated long and hard on the rewards of discipleship. They heard horrifying sermons on the agonies of hell and vivid sermons on the pleasures of heaven. They were unabashed about the rewards—writing hymns about them and speaking of them to each other. Perhaps a little more contemplation of the rewards would strengthen our faith as it strengthened theirs.

After all, who doesn't need to be motivated to do what doesn't come naturally to us with our money? We need motivation to handle our money in a way that runs contrary to the major currents of the world we live in. But once we grab hold of the fact that it is *worth it,* and *more than worth it,* to bring our approach to money under the Lord's control, what or who can keep us from believing God's word and obeying it? It's the only smart thing to do.

The books in the Living as a Christian series can be used effectively in groups. To receive a free copy of the Leader's Guide to this book and the others in the series, write to Servant Book Express, Box 8617, Ann Arbor, Michigan 48107.